GETTING I

IT and the Internet

NEIL HARRIS

TROTMAN

Getting into IT and the Internet
This first edition published in 2000
by Trotman & Company Ltd
2 The Green, Richmond, Surrey TW9 1PL

© Trotman & Company Limited 2000

British Library Cataloguing in Publication Data
A catalogue record for this book is available from the
British Library

ISBN 0 85660 549 2

Typeset by Florence Production Ltd, Stoodleigh, Devon
Printed and bound in Great Britain
by Creative Print & Design (Wales) Ltd

CONTENTS

ABOUT THE AUTHOR

Neil Harris is Director of the Careers Service at University College, London, and Deputy Director of the University of London Careers Service. His early career was in research and development in the engineering industry with GEC and IMI and at the Department of Materials Engineering, Liverpool University, where he engaged in postdoctoral research. He is the author of several publications on careers including *Getting into Engineering*, *Getting into The City*, and *Getting into Financial Services*, all published by Trotman. Neil writes a regular careers column in the *New Scientist* Magazine.

INTRODUCTION

A CHANGING WORLD

We live in an exciting age – so much of what we do and how we do it is changing. The way we communicate is moving from land-line telephone to mobile. How we access information is going from the library to the Internet. The way we receive our television signals has gone from aerials to satellite dishes and cables. Our system of buying and selling goods is changing too with the advent of a dot com society. It's a world dominated by information technology (IT) and the Internet and the only thing we can safely predict is that yet more change is on the way. No wonder then that there are so many opportunities, so many jobs and such a wealth of career development possibilities to be had in this rapidly expanding field.

According to the Information Technology National Training Organisation (ITNTO) there are at least two million people now working in IT. No one really knows how many people are involved because there are so many different degrees of involvement. Information technology and the Internet are affecting the way in which most of us work. In the past the keyboard and word-processing was the preserve of the typist. Now every top executive has their own keyboard, knows how to use it and receives and sends a continual stream of messages by e-mail. Previously we used to go into the bank and conduct our transactions through a cashier. Now we put our card into a machine and all those problems are taken care of.

The way we use telephones is perhaps the most visible aspect of the new technology. People are now using the phone in cars, walking down the street, on the bus or train. One wonders how many years it will be before the telephone box becomes a thing of the past.

The most remarkable development is the gradual convergence of three technologies – the television, the telephone and the computer. Organisations that were primarily designed to provide cable television have become telephone companies. The change to television that works with digital signals (pulses) instead of the old analogue (wave forms) system has not only improved the quality of the picture but also enabled the system to be interactive. Television sets can now be used to send and receive e-mail messages and to manage your bank account or to order your groceries. The next generation of mobile phones, using wireless application protocol (WAP), will have access to the Internet and a range of services from e-commerce to television and the retrieval of information. Personal numbers will soon be introduced that people can keep for life, irrespective of which telephone company they are using. Perhaps you even bought this book via the Internet. It will be interesting to see how the British addiction to the shopping trip survives the current onslaught of dot com buying systems.

These are just a few examples of the changes in our everyday lives that IT and the Internet are delivering. None of these changes are occurring without a vast effort. There are now so many jobs to be had, not only in the huge and growing IT industry but also in countless businesses and public sector services that now rely on these technologies. You can surely find one that fits your personality and skills. See Chapter 1.

THE SORTS OF JOBS

The first thing to appreciate is that you don't necessarily have to be a technologist to make a successful career in this area. Every telephone company, computer manufacturer or dot com organisation has people working in marketing, sales, administration, purchasing, finance, human resources and general management. If you have a clear idea of your chosen career or you have already become a professional in one, you might consider doing that job in an IT-related company, where the rapid expansion of activity is leading to increases in career potential. That said, do proceed with some caution. The current expansion of dot com companies, whose shares have been floated on the stock market at inflated prices without ever making a profit, must eventually lead to a rationalisation of the industry.

If you want to be involved with researching, designing, developing, installing, testing and using IT on a daily basis there are several areas to go into. You might be a user of software. Your job might be to maintain and use a database, perhaps to keep in touch with customers or clients, or to sell tickets for an airline or take reservations in a hotel. At a bank or accounting firm you might input figures into a spreadsheet so that accounts can be readily compiled and analysed. Working for a publisher your job could be to design the pages of a book or magazine using a publishing package. All of these jobs now require software user skills.

Another area of involvement is in the increasing number of administrative jobs associated with this technology. You might be coordinating the design of web sites for many departments in a large organisation that wants its public face to be simply excellent. Alternatively there are a growing band of workers whose job it is to update information on the web, often on a daily and sometimes on a minute-by-minute basis.

Getting more technical, you might be a computer programmer providing the software that is essential to the provision of IT and Internet services, or the systems software required to allow one piece of equipment to have meaningful contact with another.

Information technology would, of course, not be available without the vast array of equipment that is needed to sustain it. The whole edifice of IT and the Internet is built on the microprocessor, the integrated circuit on a silicon chip. Electronic engineers, working closely with software engineers, provide the heart of the system on which so many of the things we now take for granted have been built.

Communication, whether it is just a few metres or to the other side of the world, depends on networks. Networks allow your call, your e-mail or your fax to be routed from where you are to the equipment of the recipient. The design, installation and maintenance of these networks are providing yet another important source of career opportunity.

PLAN OF THE BOOK

This book is about how you get into a career in IT and the Internet and what jobs you might do when you get there. We take a detailed look at the many different kinds of job that are on offer. Several of the chapters are devoted to the career options that arise in specific areas. These include telephone companies, Internet service providers, computer and electronics manufacturers, software houses and consultants. We also investigate opportunities that can be found in industry and commerce generally.

But to achieve these careers you will need some qualifications and training. Employers are finding that there is a continuing shortage of people who possess the basic skills required to make a start in this business. Chapters 7, 8 and 9 take a detailed look at the courses of study that you can take. You won't need a degree or any high-level qualification to make a start. You can gain sufficient expertise to get a job in the industry by taking a skills-based course designed and accredited by the City & Guilds of London Institute or the OCR (Oxford, Cambridge & RSA Examinations).

We examine the courses of study, from learning how to install a computer to getting a PhD in information technology. Along the route we investigate National Vocational Qualifications (NVQs), national certificates, diplomas and degrees. Read the relevant chapters and you will soon be able to choose the level of study that is right for you and can provide the springboard for career success in IT and the Internet.

What does it take to become a fully qualified member of a professional body? Our final chapter considers the options, giving details of all the professional bodies that represent information technologists. From novice to full professional, from technocrat to working in a non-technical function, there is something for everyone.

Chapter 1
AN A TO Z OF JOBS

This chapter gives a flavour of the many different jobs that are available in IT and the Internet. They range from administrator and sales executive to systems programmer and web page designer. There are so many opportunities in this expanding industry that it is impossible to be comprehensive, but here we cover the broad generic areas. Within each of these areas there are specialisms. For example, a computer programmer could be a C++ programmer or an HTML/Java programmer. A technical consultant might be advising about interactive television or global networks. So even within each of the occupations mentioned here there is considerable variety.

Account executive

Internet service providers (ISPs) sell space on their domain to organisations. If your company wants space on their site you talk to an account executive who discusses with you what the possibilities are, how they can be implemented and the cost. Telephone service providers sell their services to targeted clients such as firms of a certain size or a particular industry. IT equipment manufacturers also sell their phones and faxes, computers, printers etc and employ account executives. A new breed of advertising agencies is growing up that specialises in helping clients to advertise on the World Wide Web. These also employ account executives. Each executive usually services a portfolio of clients that have an account – hence the name.

Skills required: Good knowledge of IT and the Internet but not necessarily technical computing skills. You must be an excellent, persuasive communicator with strong administrative abilities.

Administrator

There is a lot of administration in IT. All the dot com companies, for example, employ large numbers of people in this area. If you buy anything over the Internet it has to be physically made to happen. Whether it's a train ticket, your groceries or a book, someone has to take your order, organise the paper work and payment and get it to you.

Skills required: Sound organisational abilities and a determination to provide excellent customer support.

Analyst programmer or Programmer analyst

See Applications programmer and Systems analyst. The job includes both of these occupations.

Applications programmer (also sometimes called Software developer)

Applications programmers write the code for computer programs that provide solutions to our problems. Under this heading there are a wide range of opportunities such as writing search engines for the Internet. Whether the program is concerned with banking or manufacture, the distribution of supplies or a system to deal with airline ticket orders the computer programs have to be written.

The programming languages used change with time. In the past most business applications were written in COBOL. Now 'object-oriented' languages such as C++ are most often used. Think of it as a picture. A program is written to define each object within the picture and then the objects are all put in place to make the whole scene. The advantage of programming in this way is that programs are easier to update and maintain. If you need to change one part of the program, one of the 'objects', that can be done relatively easily without upsetting the entire system.

Creating new programs is difficult because any error, however small, will cause them not to work properly. Libraries of previously tested programs are used to increase productivity and reduce effort. Completed programs have to be tested rigorously. They are accompanied by documentation that tells those who come to update them later how they have been constructed. Coding, testing and writing documentation are all a part of this meticulous role.

(See also Software engineer.)

Skills required: Intimate knowledge and excellent ability in the key programming languages being used in your employer's environment. Logical, meticulous attention to detail, patience and persistence.

Business consultant

Business consultants work with clients of Internet service providers, information service companies and other IT industry organisations to develop IT business solutions that work and enhance their business. It is a job in which you take a detailed look at someone else's business, analyse the options and provide cost-effective, IT-based solutions.

Skills required: Excellent communication skills. Ability to deal confidently with senior staff in customer's company. Good problem solver who can provide and implement solutions that improve client's business.

Call centre agent

This is a commercial job in which the employee uses the telephone to deal with customers. Part of the work is selling IT systems, services or products. Part of it is listening to customer needs and working out how your organisation might meet them.

Skills required: Excellent interpersonal skills and ability to create instant rapport on the telephone. An overall understanding of the services that are being provided and an ability to relate these to customers in non-technical terms.

Computer operator

As with any other piece of equipment, computer systems have to be run. In the past most systems were large computers known as 'mainframes', with a computer operator in charge. Now whole networks of computers, attached to servers and memory devices, have to be organised and maintained. This is the job of the computer operator.

Skills required: Good practical skills and intimate knowledge of the system that is being operated.

Customer service engineer/executive

Buyers of complex and sophisticated products expect to be given an excellent after-sales service. People working in customer services provide the back-up they need. It may be highly technical or it could be that an administrator takes the problems and fields them to the person in the organisation best able to solve them. In software situations there are front-line customer service people and those in the second and third lines. If the first cannot solve the problem, or is too busy, it goes to number two, and if it is really difficult the third person, who is usually much more experienced, sorts it out.

Skills required: Excellent ability to put yourself in the shoes of the customer and see the problem from their point of view. Establishes rapport and has the technical skill and know-how to provide solutions.

Data analyst

Many IT applications are concerned with databases. There are databases of customers, potential customers, suppliers and employees. Car manufacturers, for example, have databases of parts, and those who supply information to the financial sector maintain databases of stocks, shares and other financial information. There are organisations, such as market research companies, which maintain large databases with vast quantities of information. Data analysts have the job of working out what information their company or client requires from a database and providing the facilities for making this happen. The way in which the database is originally set up can make it easy, or difficult, to access specific information. A well-designed database is readily analysed to provide answers to such questions as: How many of our customers live in Guildford? What has happened to BT shares over the last ten years? Is there a train from Glasgow to Edinburgh between 11am and 11.30am on Saturday? This is the domain of the data analyst.

Skills required: Strong logic and analytical skills. Attention to detail. An understanding of groups and how an item of data can belong to several groups simultaneously.

Data input clerk

There are many situations in which data must be loaded on to the computer. The data may be numbers, such as financial information or those resulting from scientific or engineering investigations; it may be words entered on a database such as the names and addresses of customers. Data input clerks have the job of inputting data and may be responsible for keeping the set of data under their control up to date. It is a job that requires endless patience and attention to detail. Another aspect of the job is when new software has been written and is being tested – data has to be put into the programs so that there is something to process.

For many this is a 'starter' job as few qualifications are required. It is more highly paid than other administrative jobs at a similar level and it provides a means of getting into the industry – a 'stepping stone' from which one can progress.

Skills required: Good keyboard skills, accuracy and meticulous attention to detail.

Database administrator

Database administrators manage complex databases, keeping them up to date and efficient. They may be responsible for the supervision of data input clerks. All documentation relating to the database, changes, maintenance and upgrades must be planned and implemented with minimum downtime.

Skills required: Good administrator with a detailed knowledge of databases plus a clear understanding of the user's requirements. Staff management skills.

Development engineer

These engineers develop a new electronic or software product from initial design to a situation where it can be produced and installed into an IT system. In electronics they have to take account of safety and economic factors. In software, speed and security may be among the issues. Can the product be made from cheaper components? Is it necessary to buy new machinery in order to produce it? Will it be attractive to customers in its proposed form? To achieve a good result development engineers have to consult widely within their organisation. They must take account of the advice of researchers and designers, the opinions of the marketing team and also their colleagues in the production department.

Skills required: Broad approach to the development of products or system. Ability to focus on the problem but at the same time think laterally about problems that may arise when it interacts with or is in competition with other products.

Electronic designer

An electrical engineer who designs circuits for electronic equipment. They might specialise in digital electronics, radio frequency systems or microwaves. The equipment being designed could be anything from a mobile phone to a satellite receiver, or a decoder that converts the signal it receives into something the next piece of equipment can make sense of. Circuits are mounted on printed circuit boards that can be changed readily when the equipment does not work correctly.

Skills required: Excellent knowledge of electronics. Practical ability to put trial systems together and then test them systematically and improve them to overcome weaknesses.

Electronic materials engineer

So important is the IT industry that it has its own brand of materials scientists and engineers, just as the metals industry always has done. When there is a requirement for a material with specific electronic properties it can be designed and produced by materials engineers: diffusing atoms of another element into them can change semiconductors; lining up tiny balls of metal and melting them can produce extremely thin wire.

Skills required: Excellent knowledge of how different materials behave and ability to choose the best one for each application. Strong practical bent for laboratory work. Persistent and painstaking in outlook.

Help desk technician

Organisations with a large network of computers – a wide area network (WAN) – need to have people running it. They usually maintain a help desk for users to approach when things go wrong. Manufacturers of computers and other IT equipment also operate help desks to give guidance for their customers, as do Internet service providers.

Those who staff help desks must have a thorough understanding of the system or product they are supporting. In some cases they can simulate the problem and go through it systematically with the user to identify what went wrong. When they are running WANs they can interrogate each user's computer to discover, for example, how much memory is taken up by the different functions.

Skills required: Intimate technical knowledge of the system. Unflappable ability to deal with users who are under stress and excellent telephone communication skills.

Installation engineer

All IT systems, whether they are servers and networks, telephone exchanges, aerials for the systems that support mobile phones or additional pieces of software, must be installed. This may involve travelling to the installation site and negotiating with managers there about what will be done and how, or it can involve installing some new software or computer system at your own offices. The work requires people who are both technically competent (though they may receive specialist training) and able to deal diplomatically with those who are affected by the installation.

Skills required: Technical ability, tact and diplomacy. Organised professional outlook.

Integrated circuit designer

Modern information technology is built on the integrated circuit. These circuits are designed to house what were previously extremely large quantities of electronic circuitry on small chips of silicon. This process is called very large scale integration (VLSI) and involves the deposition of many layers of conductor, semiconductor and insulator in prescribed patterns on to a flat surface. The technology of these processes is continually changing and the size of the components decreasing. Currently it is possible to make conducting wires that are just a few nanometres across.

Skills required: Excellent understanding of electronics in general and integrated circuits in particular. Ability to tailor-make them for specific purposes. Meticulous, logical analyst.

Internet systems developer

The Internet and its use is growing fast. Internet protocols (IPs), systems and rules for making it work have been developed and are continually being upgraded. New Internet systems are being written. Internet systems developers together with Systems architects (see below) are at the leading edge, moving the Internet on to meet greater challenges. The job involves designing novel systems that fit in with existing structures and usually includes some programming.

Skills required: Excellent knowledge of the Internet, its many uses and protocols. Creative approach to the development of novel systems.

IT salesperson

There are probably as many jobs in the selling of IT equipment as there are in its design and production. Every IT company needs sales people. Some are retailers – every high street now has shops dedicated to selling mobile telephones, computers and ancillary equipment. Numerous shops, including large retail chains, sell computers, printers, fax machines and other IT equipment.

In addition to those who sell their products and services to the public there are many who sell IT systems to businesses. This entails dealing with clients and prospective clients over the phone and meeting them face to face to promote the attractions of the products you are selling and their advantages compared with competing products.

Skills required: Excellent communication and persuasive skills. Logical approach to customers' problems. Ability to establish easy rapport and develop long-term customer relationships.

IT trainer

Such is the pace of development in IT that we all need regular training just to keep up with new technology. For most of us this means coming to grips with a new piece of software, perhaps for word-processing or databases, for publishing or for using the Internet more efficiently. IT trainers provide the teaching we need to keep our IT skills up to date. Some are employed in IT training establishments and others work for the makers of IT products that provide training in the use of their new products as part of their service to customers. Large organisations, which have extensive IT needs, employ their own trainers.

Skills required: Deep understanding of IT systems and an ability to explain them in simple terms to those who wish to learn. Tact and patience plus excellent communication and interpersonal skills are required.

Media buyer

Employed in an advertising agency to buy space for advertisements. Advertising locations include television, radio, newspapers and journals, hoardings, taxis, station platforms, even waste bins in the high street. Everywhere we look these days we see advertising of IT equipment and services. Media buyers working in this field understand where their typical customers are likely to see the adverts and buy space accordingly. The Internet is a new advertising medium and there are agencies that specialise in assisting clients to advertise there.

Skills required: Excellent telephone manner and ability to negotiate over the phone with media suppliers. An understanding of the advertisements to be placed and how to gain the maximum audience response.

Multimedia producer

Multimedia systems are often produced on CD-ROMs that include text, photographs, video, numerical data, pictures and drawings. It takes a particular skill to arrange all of this in a logical sequence so that they all come together to give a coherent message. Some of these systems are interactive, and when used in training are often produced under the direction of a skilled trainer or teacher (see IT trainer).

Skills required: The ability to prepare several different media on the same subject and compile a program. Creativity plus sequential logic are required.

Network manager

Most IT applications are run on networks. They may be local area networks (LANs) that cover all the employees in a firm or global networks for telephone systems. Alternatively they can be wide area networks dedicated to a particular user, such as a bank. Automatic telling machines (ATMs), the high street cash machines, are an example of a system run on a network. Network managers are responsible for their continuous operation, and it is their responsibility to implement any maintenance or upgrading, any extension geographically or change of use.

Skills required: Excellent technical knowledge of how the network operates, both the software and hardware involved. Management skills to supervise engineers or technicians who may be working on the detailed problems of the network.

Project manager

A person who manages a project team. In an IT environment this might be one that is tasked with designing and developing the next generation of mobile phones or interactive television systems. Project managers must have a clear understanding of their goal and the steps that must be taken to achieve it. Theirs is the responsibility for deciding how to utilise the resources at their disposal in terms of staffing, equipment and finance.

Skills required: Strong management skills. Deep understanding of the technology of the project. A clear vision of what they want to achieve and the ability to communicate that to their staff.

Radio frequency/Microwave engineer

The development of mobile phones has led to a huge increase in demand for radio frequency and microwave engineers, this being the part of the radio spectrum employed in that method of communication. They too are concerned with electronic design, but also the design of transmitters and receivers. Mobile phone operators rely on a cellular system of masts spread across the country that ensure mobile phone users can receive and send messages. These engineers are also concerned with the design, production and maintenance of these facilities.

Skills required: An in-depth understanding of radio frequency technology and the ability to apply it in the design and development of new wireless systems.

Software developer

See Applications programmer, which is a different title for the same job.

Software engineer

Software engineers are programmers. The term is most often used in the electronics industry, where software regularly has a part to play in electronic circuits. When circuits are being designed some of their functions are achieved electronically and others by using software, which helps the equipment to make decisions. People who write these programs are usually called software engineers.

Software engineering is also the term used to describe a rigorous method of programming that puts software together block by block, just as you might engineer a product. Using this approach it is easier to discover where things are going wrong (when they do) and much simpler to maintain and update the software when required.

Skills required: Logical and analytical, with a meticulous attention to detail and an ability to build software in a systematic way so that it is readily maintained and updated.

Systems administrator

Systems administrators deal with all the problems that arise on a system and get them sorted. They monitor and record what goes wrong. When development teams have new systems to be installed they ensure that the process is carried out smoothly and at minimum inconvenience to users. They keep meticulous records on each change and upgrade to the system so that the cause of faults can be readily diagnosed.

Skills required: An in-depth knowledge of the system that is being administered. Excellent administration and communication skills. You need to be able to work well under pressure.

Systems analyst

Systems analysts analyse systems that need to be computerised. It might be a share dealing system where every deal is recorded and documents produced or a university entrance system that tracks the applications of each person to several universities. Whatever the system it is analysed systematically in terms of where information comes from, how it is processed and where it then goes at every stage. This is a precursor to the programming, sometimes called coding.

Skills required: Analytical and logical plus the ability to communicate with people who run the system that is to be altered.

Systems architect

Systems architects are at the forefront of new developments in technology, especially on the Internet. They understand all the latest technologies and are the architects of new systems and technologies that meet their customers' needs.

Skills required: Excellent knowledge of a broad range of technologies and the ability to apply them to any problem that arises. The communication skills required to gain a clear understanding of clients' needs and inform them about what is possible and how it is to be achieved.

Systems engineer/Systems developer

These engineers work on IT systems, taking them from initial concept through to implementation. The system may use many different technologies, each of which the systems engineer/developer must master. As the system develops it has to be tested in a realistically simulated situation so that each function is known to work properly before it goes 'live'.

Skills required: Strong and broad technical knowledge. Patience to build new systems and iron out the flaws. Creative problem solver.

17

Systems programmer

Systems programmers write the software that helps the computer system to work efficiently. On the Internet this is an important contribution, allowing the system to operate and receive thousands of users all at the same time. Systems programs allow each piece of equipment within the IT system to send and receive messages from the rest. The computer can tell the printer to print, for example, or switch on the telephone line to get on to the World Wide Web. Systems programs are written in low-level languages more easily understood by the computer than the 4GLs (fourth-generation languages) used in applications programming.

Skills required: Methodical, analytical problem solver.

Technical consultant

Technical consultants are people with at least five years' experience in the IT industry who advise others by using their skills in a particular area. Often they possess knowledge in a niche area that is useful to their colleagues in the same organisation. Alternatively they may be working as consultants for external clients, advising them for example of the steps required to get into e-business.

Skills required: Excellent technical ability. Problem solver with good communication skills and the ability to understand clients' needs and provide solutions.

Test engineer

When electronic equipment has been produced and is rolling off the production line it has to be tested. This is the job of test engineers. The high level of sophistication of electronic equipment makes this a time-consuming task. Test engineers often have or design and make special pieces of equipment that will carry out an automatic test and highlight any deficiencies. In software, engineers test the many different routes through the program to ensure that they all work as expected.

Skills required: Systematic diagnostic skills. Persistence and patience plus a good understanding of the technology.

Web site designer

Every business now needs a web site. One day it was the preserve of the few, now it's almost an essential piece of kit for running a successful business. Individuals have web sites too, including the Queen and the Prime Minister. So there are a great many opportunities for people to design web sites.

Some sites are flashy, with moving parts, and others are plain. When you visit a flashy one it takes so long to download you wish you hadn't bothered. Web site designers think about colours and logos, how many pages are required to get the information across and how the viewer will get from one part of the site to another. Many have links that take you to other relevant web pages. They use the Java and HTML programming languages or a piece of software kit known as 'Front Page'.

Some web sites are designed by consultants, others by people in the IT department of an organisation. A few are produced by non-IT people who just need enough information, tools and knowledge to learn how to design their own site. Quite inexperienced people can use software packages, such as Front Page, specifically designed for this purpose. Web sites need to be updated regularly, otherwise the organisation soon looks very foolish. They can be openly accessible to anyone or restricted to those who have a password or are members of an Intranet. Some web site consultants advertise regular updates as part of their package.

Skills required: Ability to communicate with clients and create novel designs on screen. Understanding of basic web structures and technologies.

Web site manager/coordinator

Large organisations have numerous web sites. There might be one for each department, product or project. Organisations value their image and want to protect it, so the web site is an essential part of public relations and a web site coordinator may be appointed. Their job is to oversee the entire set of sites belonging to an organisation, set out guidelines or rules for what is and is not considered acceptable practice and ensure that these are adhered to. As the situation develops they control the 'home page', which provides directions about how to access the rest.

Skills required: Sound administrative skills and ability to liaise between a range of interested parties.

Writer and editor

So much material is now required for the information pages on the World Wide Web that there are writers and editors involved in providing it. The monitor screen is a slightly different shape to the page of a book and is often subdivided into more than one vertical column, so the requirements are slightly different in terms of content, layout and presentation to those of books, magazines and newspapers. The British Army, for example, has a recruitment web site that extends to 4000 pages. That's a lot of writing and editing.

Skills required: Excellent writing skills and an understanding of what can be achieved in the different media.

Chapter 2
CAREERS WITH TELEPHONE SERVICE COMPANIES

THE EMPLOYERS

Telephone services in Europe used to be owned by the state, every country having its own. Over the last 15 years there has been a transformation from inefficient monopolies that had little interest outside their own borders to highly sophisticated competitive global businesses. While the top players in the market such as BT, Cable and Wireless, AT&T, Vodafone Airtouch, Deutsche Telekom, MCI Worldcom and NTL are well known, hundreds of organisations now have a licence to provide telephone services here in the UK. All are employers. The cable television company NTL has been rapidly acquiring others to become a major player in the telephone services market. Energis was born when the National Grid discovered that power lines could be used to transmit telephone messages.

Early in 2000 the UK government invited companies to bid for licences to provide mobile telephone services. BT Cellnet, TIW, One to One, Vodafone and Orange were the winners. Having produced £22 million for the UK Treasury this process is expected to be repeated elsewhere, starting in Germany.

Increasing competition and rapid developments in technology are delivering an ever-increasing array of services to the customer. The telephone service companies are also becoming Internet service providers. BT, for example, now has BT Click, an Internet Service. BT Openworld, another offering from BT, provides continuous access to the Internet, without logging on or off, in return for a monthly fee. The company is one of many that are actively selling e-commerce solutions to its business customers, large and small. The next generation of mobile phones, known as 3G (third generation) and using wireless application protocol (WAP), will be like a palmtop computer, an Internet access point and a television set all rolled into one.

For now we have automatic answering of calls, sounds that tell us someone is trying to interrupt our current call, indications that tell us where a call is coming from and the ability to have a conference call. These have all emerged among the competitive services. Following the introduction of Freeserve the heat is on for telephone service companies to provide Internet services at very low prices (see Chapter 3).

THE SORTS OF JOBS

So where are the jobs in the telephone service organisations? First there are jobs in *research and development*. BT, for example, has a research establishment at Martelsham, near Ipswich, where electronic and telecommunications engineers, plus people with qualifications in other subjects (including physics and materials science) research how to deliver the telecommunications systems of the future. A key development is asymmetric digital subscriber lines (ADSLs) that allow up to 40 times more information to be passed down the same copper cable than the previous systems such as ISDN. In the past services such as video could not be delivered because they took up more space than was available. Now receiving video on computers and mobile phones will soon be a standard feature. Researchers are forecasting future demand (which will escalate dramatically as we all get on the web) and working out how the networks must be developed to meet it.

Engineers and scientists working for telephone service companies consider new services, and where they are commercially attractive they work out how to make them happen. Some are employed as *software architects and designers* to conceive the overall plan of a new system and develop the operating software. They decide the specification of the structure that will support sustainable developments and be robust enough to deal with the expected throughput.

Everything is now moving rapidly from analogue (wave form) to digital (pulses). Every piece of information, whether a picture, text or video, can be expressed in digital form – that's the job of *digital designers*.

Mobile phones are essentially wirelesses that use broadband radio frequency waves. Telephone service companies are competing frantically for *radio frequency developers*, who are in short supply. Their job is to transform the mobile phone into a palmtop notebook that can deliver a whole range of new services. *Multimedia designers* are also recruited, whose job it is to research and develop interactive multimedia systems.

Keeping the entire networks operational are *customer service engineers*. They are the people who check faults at telephone exchanges, or dash up a ladder to investigate the wiring to a telegraph pole. They visit customers' premises to get equipment up and running or service the large number of masts that are now seen all over the country providing a cellular network for mobile phones. In some companies, such as Cable and Wireless, *field engineers* installing the networks have direct contacts with the equipment suppliers (see Chapter 4).

A large number of people in the industry have the job of finding solutions to customers' problems. This is a vast and growing area of employment. *Sales executives and consultants* are talking to customers about the networks they need and *network engineers* are working out how to supply these services. Others are engaged in providing video conference services. Changes in the delivery of and payment for Internet services has brought in a range of people who are actively *selling* e-business systems to even quite small businesses.

In marketing departments competitive *business strategists* are needed. *Market research* is being carried out to predict the flow of traffic; loyalty schemes and pricing structures are continually being updated, *advertising* campaigns are organised and put into action. *Procurement* is another important area. Close contact with equipment producers is essential to provide the means of developing networks, installing exchanges, servers and phones. *Human resource managers* have to compete in an intense market where there is a dire shortage of people with the skills the companies require. *Accountants* are also regularly recruited for busy finance departments.

For details of what these jobs entail please refer to Chapter 1. All the companies have web sites and most post their vacancies on them. Some have a complete electronic system for applicants, who can complete applications on the web and e-mail them to the companies.

A KEY PLAYER

Last year BT, still the UK market leader in telecommunication services and owner of Cellnet, recruited over 700 graduates and apprentices, sponsored more than 200 students through its placement scheme and also awarded several research fellowships to senior researchers. The range of qualifications of its recruits vary from GCSEs to PhDs, and while some joiners have no previous experience others come with several years' experience within the industry. The company, in common with the rest of the industry, recruits people into a very broad range of jobs.

QUALIFICATIONS AND QUALITIES REQUIRED

To make a career in this fast-changing environment you don't have to be a technologist. Many of the jobs are for people without technical qualifications, especially those in sales, project management, procurement and finance and administration. It is important, however, to have a personality that fits the company. BT seeks employees who fit their carefully chosen recruitment criteria. Aspiring employees need drive and enthusiasm and the ability to thrive in changing situations. They must not only manage themselves but also motivate others. The ability to communicate well, particularly about technical details, is also significant. Successful applicants are customer focused, good team players and capable of generating ideas. If you intend to apply to a telephone service company think carefully how you can persuade their recruitment managers that you have these skills by indicating when you applied them in practice.

Chapter 3
CAREERS WITH INTERNET SERVICE PROVIDERS

THE EMPLOYERS

Just as there are hundreds of telephone companies there are also numerous Internet service providers (ISPs – see the list at the end of this chapter). Freeserve shook the market by offering free access to the Internet and gained 1.5 million customers in no time at all. Cable television and telephone company NTL responded by offering free Internet services to its customers. BT are now offering continual access to the Internet – no logging on or off – for a monthly fee. So surfing the net is getting cheaper and the percentage of the population using it is increasing rapidly. Companies are also using the Internet for commercial purposes in ever-increasing numbers and advertising on the net is becoming big business, just as it has been on television and in the newspapers.

Working for an ISP is both exciting and demanding. It is like working for a newspaper, a publisher, a software house, a large supermarket (virtual of course) and a telephone company all rolled into one. Because the business is developing, often in unexpected ways, the range of jobs is also expanding. It is no longer a place just for the technical boffin, if ever it was.

How does it work? Demon Internet, one of the oldest and largest operators, began trading in 1992. Demon's engineers and scientists continually improved how Demon works and today it has massive computer power and dedicated transatlantic telephone lines capable of carrying 45 megabytes of information at the same time. It was the company that first established a system by which you can dial into an Internet service provider anywhere for the price of a local telephone call.

Internet service providers talk about bandwidth and connectivity – can you actually get through to them or are they often engaged? Their software and hardware experts are continually expanding the equipment to meet increasing demand. They are also providing new services. Demon offers its clients web hosting – meaning that its web site is continually available on the Demon hub. It sells e-commerce solutions to companies and security systems to give them credibility. Clients can have their web pages specially designed and, of course, for us the browsers there is Internet connection and the e-mail service.

There may be lots of information on the net but you may well need a search engine such as Yahoo! to discover where it is. So as well as the ISPs there are also numerous other companies devising software that provides other services such as browsers and search engines, auction systems and systems that allow you to buy with confidence that your credit card number is secure.

Globix is one of the companies that designs software solutions for the web. With offices in London, New York and Santa Clara they recruit new graduates as Internet technology associates and sales consultants and provide them with two months' professional training. It provides many of the services of an ISP but also Globix Streaming Media digitises video pictures and sends them around the world via the Internet.

THE SORTS OF JOBS

IT experts working for the ISPs tend to be highly qualified and experienced. Most recruit their staff from other software companies rather than train them up from scratch. Perhaps this will change when graduates start rolling out of the new Internet degree courses (see Chapter 8).

Typical technical jobs include *network engineers* who keep the ISPs' networks running and expanding to meet demand. They visit leading clients to ensure that they are always able to be online. Currently these engineers are usually people with at least two years' experience and an understanding of Internet protocols, expertise in Windows NT plus a few programming languages including Perl and HTML.

Web developers are also in demand. They develop the ISP site plus the web sites of their clients and need to be experienced in the UNIX operating system plus C++ and the other languages just mentioned. There are also employees providing *technical support* for customers who phone the help line. An understanding of how business servers work and some knowledge of Windows are essential skills for their particular role. That's how it is now, of course, and tomorrow it could be quite different.

Think of the ISP as an advertising agency and you will also realise they need *account managers* and *graphic designers*. The account managers bring in the business from a portfolio of clients, selling the services that are available, including the advertising. Graphic designers, just like in advertising agencies, actually make the adverts. But there is a difference. They too need to use HTML plus the odd bit of software such as Photoshop, Flash and animation packages.

Think next of the ISP as a retailer with lots of e-commerce sites where people can buy their books, their groceries, organise their mortgage and so much more. Security is a major problem. In Chapter 9 we discuss postgraduate degrees in computer security systems. These people are very necessary. If the ISP got a reputation for selling e-commerce software solutions that were open to fraud it would soon close down.

In addition to these employees the Internet generates great quantities of *administration*, so there is always room for people who can meticulously organise or invent a novel administrative system. And every ISP has to *market* itself competitively in order to win clients. They all have marketing professionals, checking what the competition is doing, looking at charges, and introducing incentives for customers and browsers.

As the dot com revolution rolls on, the business will undoubtedly change. But it's definitely here to stay and it will definitely be growing. Those who got in at the start could find that their careers move upwards with the Internet, but there will be plenty of room for others to join in the party later.

SOME ISPs

- Aardvaak
- America Online (AOL)
- BT Internet
- Claranet
- Compuserve
- Demon Internet
- Easynet
- Enterprise

- 4unet
- FirstWeb
- Free Online
- Freeserve
- Netcom
- Paradise Internet
- Saq Internet
- Virgin Net

Chapter 4
WORKING FOR MANUFACTURERS OF IT EQUIPMENT

THE EQUIPMENT

At the very core of IT and the Internet is the equipment. Without it we would achieve nothing. The whole IT world is built upon the microprocessor, a 'chip' of silicon on which is deposited minute electronic circuits. Over the last 20 years these 'chips' have been able to include ever more circuitry on to a smaller area. Other materials, including germanium, have also been used. As a result of this microcircuitry the size of computers, telephones and other equipment has shrunk dramatically. Now the minimum size of some equipment is limited not by what's inside but by the size of the button one can press to input data.

The equipment includes the electronic systems, the memory devices, microprocessors, computers, modems, faxes, printers, servers, cables (optical or copper) and networks. It also includes telephone exchanges, telephones (mobile and fixed), pagers and much, much more.

Old telephone communication systems used to rely on analogue technology. Each signal was represented by a wave of electrons, and each wave had a different shape. Now we use digital electronics in which pulses of electrons provide the signals. Some systems also use opto-electronics, based on lasers sending signals down optical fibres. A system known as asymmetric digital subscriber line (ADSL), using old copper cables, is currently being rolled out that provides up to 40 times the capacity of previous data transmission methods. These developments make it possible to send more signals simultaneously down the same wire or fibre than ever before. When you think of a world in which most people are using the Internet the number of messages that can be sent and received at any one time through the network of wires, fibres and cables is absolutely crucial.

A way around this problem is to dispense with wires and use microwaves. Everyone can have their own mobile phone that can send and receive messages, which are transmitted to a local mast. These are springing up all over the country, and since mobile phone companies don't share these facilities, but must each have their own network of masts, there are huge numbers of ugly edifices littering our countryside, towns and cities.

Now we are using all of these systems. If you contact someone on their fixed, wired-in telephone using your mobile phone, the signal will start as a microwave and end as a digital electronic one. In the other direction the opposite happens. The interconnection between all these technologies that makes them compatible with each other is an essential part of modern telephone systems.

Satellites and sub-sea cables also play an important role, making it possible to talk just as easily to people on the other side of the world as you can to those in the same street.

THE EMPLOYERS

For each piece of equipment there is a range of manufacturers. Those that make mobile phones include Nokia, Philips and Ericsson; those that make the original electronic components include Intel, Texas Instruments, Marconi, Motorola and Smiths Industries. Matra Marconi produces communication satellites and has them placed in orbit. Marconi makes telephone exchanges. IBM, ICL, Hewlett Packard and many more make computers. These are some of the employers. What do you do if you're working for them?

THE SORTS OF JOBS

First there are jobs in the *design* of new electronic circuits. People who design, develop, produce, test and maintain equipment tend to have qualifications in electronics, physics or materials science. A few are chemists and mechanical engineers. In some pieces of equipment, particularly mobile phones, effects produced by one electronic component can affect the operation of another. So it is not simply a question of designing a circuit that works, it also has to be one that fits easily into the available space and function with the components all in close proximity.

Chemists and materials scientists work on the development of electronic materials, those used to make components such as semiconductors, resistors and integrated circuits.

Modern electronic systems usually include software, computer programs stored in a memory device that help the circuit to decide what to do in a range of different situations. *Software engineers*, who work closely with *electronic engineers*, so that each part of the circuit readily integrates with the rest and everything they want the circuit to achieve is included, design these programmes. Electronic engineers are involved in every step along the way, from the design and development of a new circuit to the whole product. The design and manufacture of external casing for computers, telephones etc in plastic or metal is the job of *mechanical engineers*.

When the method of production has been worked out and all the necessary pieces have been purchased, *engineers* oversee production systems, maintaining the plant and testing the final products. Introducing new pieces of equipment into a production line, arranging computer control of manufacturing units and maintaining equipment in good working condition is an essential part of the job. Some electronic production systems also include robots, another product of the information technology era, which move parts automatically to where they are required.

Testing sophisticated equipment, such as new computers, is by no means a simple task because there are so many different ways in which it can be used. Specialist systems have to be designed and made for this purpose alone.

Most people who buy IT equipment do not have any idea of how it actually works. They don't need to. But they insist on a high quality back-up service for when things go wrong. The first line of customer service is often a telephone-based *customer help line*, staffed by engineers who have a detailed understanding of the product and can often get customers' equipment up and working by giving sound and immediate advice. Should that approach fail, engineers have to visit the customer to repair the equipment or have it sent in for servicing. Again there are numerous opportunities for qualified people to work in this area.

A few engineers move from the technical specialities to the more commercial areas of *technical marketing and sales, purchasing and supply chain management* and the *recruitment* of technically qualified staff.

It is not only in the private sector that these technical skills are prized. Government agencies including the Defence Evaluation and Research Agency (DERA) and the Government Communications Headquarters (GCHQ) are among public bodies that rely heavily on IT and the Internet. The Army's Royal Signals regiment is another. IT is an essential weapon in defence. The ability to provide secure communications systems, to pinpoint enemy targets, to provide excellent navigation and guidance systems for ships, jets, missiles and torpedoes are of paramount importance.

SOME OF THE KEY PLAYERS

Mitel Semiconductor designs and makes semiconductor devices at its plants in Lincoln, Oldham, Swindon and Plymouth, and abroad. They produce thin wafers of material to include in integrated circuits. Materials scientists, physicists, electronic engineers and computer scientists are among their most important recruits to work both in design and in the production of products.

Hewlett Packard designs, makes, sells and services electronic equipment, including printers and computers. The company recruits people with similar qualifications to Mitel for jobs in research and development, engineering, production, marketing and sales. Trainee engineers receive six weeks' technical training on Hewlett Packard products in the USA followed by secondment to different departments back home in the UK to extend and broaden their knowledge and commercial awareness.

Nortel boasts that it is the 'world's leading supplier of fully digital telecommunications equipment'. The company recruits trainees with qualifications in electronics, telecommunications and computer science as well as graduates from other disciplines for the less technical aspects of its business. It develops and maintains European wireless networks and systems to transmit data voice and other material for its clients.

Nokia, with headquarters in Finland, is established in 45 countries worldwide where it pursues its two main businesses of mobile phones and telecommunications. The company is a leading supplier of GSM-based cellular networks and of mobile phones. It provides transmission systems, multimedia equipment, satellite and cable receivers. 'We are particularly interested in people who have qualifications in engineering, technology, computing, physics and telecommunications,' says the company.

The old GEC, historically one of the largest UK IT equipment suppliers, was broken up in 1999 and the telephone business became Marconi, which is now an international provider of telephone equipment and exchanges. The company regularly recruits over 100 graduates every year, most with HND or degree qualifications in electronic engineering, computer science or related disciplines such as physics and mechanical engineering.

Chapter 5
WORKING FOR SOFTWARE HOUSES AND CONSULTANTS

THE EMPLOYERS

There are numerous firms of software and systems houses, whose business is to provide solutions for their clients' IT problems. Some are large international companies such as Cap Gemini, Logica, EDS and Andersen Consulting. Such organisations have the workforce to bid for very big projects because they employ many thousands of people worldwide. Andersen Consulting, for example, employs 40,000 people in 152 offices located in 47 countries. At the other end of the scale are quite small software firms, some employing fewer than 20 people. The Computing Services and Software Association (CSSA, the trade organisation of software houses) has over 420 member and affiliated firms, all of which provide software and systems consultancy for their clients. They provide services in a very wide range of areas, from help desk systems to software for image processing and project management. Some develop programming methodologies and network management software. The range of activities is extensive.

The big organisations tend to operate in divisions, each specialising in a different area of the economy – finance, defence, the public sector, manufacturing and so on. The smaller concerns usually focus on a niche market such as packages for medical records, point-of-sale systems in shops or software to assist doctors with medical records or personnel departments with applicants' details.

Two different activities emerge. The first is the provision of software tailor-made to a particular client's needs. Andersen Consulting, for example, provided systems for the Benefits Agency so that they could keep track of those claiming benefit and be sure that they do not do so at several different offices. Second is the production of generic software packages that can be sold to a range of different clients but for a similar purpose. Microsoft is certainly the market leader in that field.

A third activity is the running of IT services for companies that do not wish to run their own. Some see advantages in getting in an external expert organisation that has fully qualified and trained staff readily available to do this. It is an activity called 'facilities management' by some and 'business operations management' by others. Whatever its name this was an area of huge growth for software and systems houses during the latter half of the last decade.

Software and systems houses vary in their employment policies. Some take only those with relevant IT and Internet qualifications. Others look for the brightest people they can find and train them in IT from scratch. Yet more only recruit people who have already had some relevant experience in their industry. A few provide extensive initial training. At PricewaterhouseCoopers and Andersen Consulting this can be up to eight weeks' training during the first year of employment, given to all recruits. Others design the training to meet each individual's training need, so everyone does not undertake the same courses.

THE SORTS OF JOBS

There is a range of occupations. Recruits often start as *trainee programmers*, sometimes called *associate consultants*. After initial training they are allocated to a project where they are engaged in coding computer programs.

Working on projects trainees learn to develop programs, often building them to include previously used software taken from libraries. Once the code is written it is tested by inputting realistic data and checking that the software works as it should. Programmers design and produce screens of information that provide the interface between the user and the software and logical systems for moving from one part of the software to another.

Later they begin to *manage* teams of programmers and *liaise* with the client to analyse what is required. With a few years' experience many programmers begin to talk to clients about their proposed systems and become *analyst programmers*. Then the job includes analysing problems in detail. When the analysis is complete and the routes for information flow and processing have been defined, *systems analysts* break down problems into small manageable chunks and give each programmer some of it to put into computer code. This definition includes understanding at each logical step where information comes from, how it will be processed and where it will then go. They have to be aware of the quantity of data that will be transmitted and stored when a particular application is working so that the computer system is designed to cope with this.

Project managers lead project teams and liaise with their clients at every stage to ensure that projects are completed to the customers' requirements. They must deliver the new system on time and within budget, by managing their teams effectively. Documentation is produced at every stage so that the specification of a new system is clear. When the project comes to a successful conclusion the client's staff may need to be trained in how to use the system and ongoing customer support supplied when faults occur or upgrading and maintenance is necessary.

The large software consultancies take on work throughout the world and employees can find themselves working on projects either in different parts of the country or abroad. Junior programmers can further their career in a chosen direction by getting to know the project leaders whose work interests them and seeking a place on their teams.

As people change teams after every project, and in some cases during long projects, their responsibilities and status vary. An employee might take a leading role in one project and a supporting role in another. This flexibility is an important aspect of life in any project-related environment.

Consultants are the people who discuss new business with their clients, define in general terms what has to be achieved and write proposals for new business. Everyone in IT consultancy has to move ahead as technology advances, so continuous training is essential. Currently many are working on e-commerce systems for which there is overwhelming demand.

The other side of the business is the *management of IT systems* for other companies. In this situation the role is one of managing and maintaining computer systems and keeping them continually updated. The range of work includes operating the computer network, inputting data, providing a help desk and emergency assistance for the users and sometimes training the client's staff to cope with new systems. Based at the client's premises people working in such an environment integrate with their client's employees, and provide services as the need arises in the business.

SOME OF THE KEY PLAYERS

Cap Gemini looks for graduates who have an upper second-class degree or better, preferably in an IT-related discipline, maths, sciences, business or law. Recruits, who do not necessarily have any programming experience, spend their first six weeks at the Cap Gemini Academy learning technical, interpersonal and business skills before being assigned to a project team.

At CMG, another international firm with offices in the Netherlands, Germany, France, Belgium and the UK, recruits are expected to already possess some programming experience. A numerate IT-related or science degree is expected and those with little experience go on a three-month intensive training programme.

Data Connection, by contrast, is a smaller organisation specialising in software for computer manufacturers. They recruit graduates from any discipline and don't expect them to have any prior computing experience.

Andersen Consulting recruits well-qualified people from a wide range of backgrounds, often without any IT skills. Initial training is six weeks long and during that time recruits learn all they need to know to become a useful member of a team.

Many of the employers give aspiring applicants an aptitude test to complete under severe time pressures. The test includes questions in verbal, numerical and diagrammatic reasoning. Several books are available that will give you an idea of what they are after (see 'Further reading').

Chapter 6
APPLYING IT AND THE INTERNET IN BUSINESS

USES OF IT

Everywhere one looks there are people working in IT and the Internet. Almost every business activity uses computers. Every firm of any size will soon have its own web site and pages, its own e-mail addresses and its own e-commerce systems developed to sell goods and services internationally though the Internet.

We mentioned in Chapter 5 that some organisations use external IT consultants to run their IT systems for them but the majority have to organise their own affairs and recruit people for that purpose. Here are a few of the many different uses of IT in business:

- communicating both internally and externally
- running the payroll
- keeping accounts
- maintaining databases of customers and suppliers
- mailing potential clients
- designing products
- controlling manufacturing equipment
- organising a supply chain
- publishing marketing material
- drawing up a timetable or room booking system
- modelling business conditions
- analysing data or scientific results
- researching information via the Internet
- advertising through web pages
- selling through e-commerce.

Most organisations have an IT or technology department to push forward these uses, which increase the efficiency and effectiveness of their business. Using the Internet even quite small firms can have an international presence, something that was unthinkable only ten years ago.

WHAT THE JOBS ENTAIL

What do people in the technology, or IT department do? First they must maintain a local area network – a system of computers all linked to each other, and via telephone to the outside world, that enables everyone within their organisation to communicate both internally and externally. In large organisations these systems have to be maintained 24 hours a day. During the working day, at least, a help line must be staffed so that users who experience difficulties can get assistance when something goes wrong. This system may be an internally secure intranet that does not allow external competitors to see what is going on.

One of the functions of the IT department is to introduce new software and often to provide training for other staff in its use. They listen to the requirements of managers and suggest ways in which these can be achieved.

Large firms usually have web sites that must be maintained and kept up to date. Small organisations may use specialist external consultants for this purpose, big organisations sometimes do it themselves. Large companies and public sector organisations often need a web site for each of their departments. Then it becomes necessary to employ a web site manager, to insist that each department portray itself in a manner that is consistent with the image of the rest of the company. Public relations and image become important issues in this. The use of logos is important and rules have to be drawn up to ensure consistency.

Imagine a marketing department that wants to advertise their new products on the web, or a personnel department that wishes applicants for jobs to complete their application forms electronically. These are both projects for the IT department, but if they cannot cope with the pressure of work external consultants will be hired.

THE EMPLOYERS

Banks all have large IT departments. In retail banks they provide computer systems to operate hole in the wall cash machines (ATMs), and to calculate your statement and interest or dividends electronically. There are machines that read and process cheques. International investment banks operate global computer networks (wide area networks). They have the technology to process information and transmit it from country to country. For each of the financial products they are trading, whether they are derivatives or equities, bonds or currencies, there are IT systems to finalise the deal and provide all the paperwork. Information companies such as Reuters provide up to the minute on-screen information (often financial) for their client companies.

Oil companies and engineering concerns are also among those that use IT extensively. At Bacton, near Great Yarmouth, there are control rooms that use telecommunication systems to operate oil wells way out at sea. Modelling oil fields from seismic and other data to calculate the optimum way to extract the oil and estimate the output is just one example. Simulating distribution systems to optimise their operation and using artificial intelligence to control chemical plant at oil refineries are just a few other IT applications.

Another use of IT is in supply chain management. When we visit our supermarket and check out the goods at the till the act of flashing the bar code over the bleeper makes the computer calculate a reduction in the stock. When stock levels reach a predetermined point more stock is automatically called up from regional warehouses and further up the chain additional supplies are ordered. Without IT this would be an extremely time-consuming job and one that could not be achieved with the precision required to run retail operations seven days a week, and in some cases 24 hours a day.

There are, of course, countless other examples: all the airlines operate computer systems to organise their booking and ticketing activities. Theatres and many of the larger hotels work in a similar way for seat and room reservations. Personnel departments increasingly receive applications by e-mail on forms that are made available on the World Wide Web for completion.

41

Engineering organisations use IT to help them with their design work, optimising systems and electronically controlling equipment. Providers of geophysical services use IT in the collection, processing and interpretation of the data they collect. It's an IT world in which more applications of the advancing technology come along so rapidly that it is difficult for most of us to keep abreast of it all.

SOME OF THE KEY PLAYERS

Who then are the major recruits in this sector?

Shell, the oil company, for one. Not only does it do all the things mentioned in the paragraph above about oil, it is also a major retailer, running shops at each of its service stations. Additionally Shell's IT department provides consultancy services to firms in other industries. When recruiting Shell looks for employees with IT-related qualifications who can demonstrate a track record of personal achievement and initiative. One activity in which Shell is typical is in running its own intranet – a secure IT network that can only be accessed by employees who have a certain password. Most organisations don't want their competitors to know every detail of their business plans, so they use an intranet to pass information within the organisation instead of the open World Wide Web.

Marks & Spencer is typical of recruiters in the retail sector, where John Lewis and Sainsbury are also among those with extensive IT departments. They recruit employees from a wide range of backgrounds, including graduates from any degree discipline, and give them a thorough training in IT. 'After initial training as a systems developer,' say M&S, 'you can remain technically based – design, develop an analytical bias in an area such as business systems, or combine these skills with managerial responsibilities as a project manager.'

Glaxo Wellcome employs 2500 people worldwide in its information systems departments. Trainees take one of two routes. Some join the 'information technology management scheme', which gives three years of training including projects and placements in every part of the business – research and development, marketing, finance and manufacturing. Trainees apply IT to problems in planning, manufacturing, business analysis and project management. Another route is recruitment to Glaxo Wellcome's worldwide information systems architecture and technology organisation. This role helps to ensure that GW's businesses across the world can communicate information and that each local operation has systems that match the requirements of the global business.

Chapter 7
QUALIFICATIONS IN IT: THE BASICS

STARTING OUT

Once you decide that you want to make your career in information technology and the Internet there are lots of courses available that will help you to increase your knowledge and develop the skills you need to make your career a success. Some are short courses that help you to understand something quite specific, such as becoming proficient in the use of a particular piece of software or learning to program computers in a certain language. Studies in that category are validated by the City & Guilds of London Institute (CGLI) and the OCR (Oxford, Cambridge & RSA Examinations) and can be studied at colleges of further education all over the UK. They are also offered by numerous private tutorial organisations such as Pitmans. The names and addresses of organisations in your area that offer the opportunity to study such courses can be found in your local Yellow Pages under the heading 'Computer training'. In London *Floodlight* is the publication that provides details of training and study opportunities, both full and part time.

Some suppliers of equipment and software also provide training that gives people an expertise with specific products. Microsoft, for example, validates courses that result in a certificate as a Microsoft Certified Engineer. The holder of such a qualification is guaranteed to be adept in the use of certain products. These qualifications can be useful for those without other formal qualifications who want to get a toe-hold in the IT industry, but they are confined to expertise in the products listed on the certificate and don't necessarily provide the students with a broad understanding of IT or the Internet. Without further qualifications, and a broader understanding, the flexibility of one's career development may be restricted.

Formal academic qualifications start at GCSE and go up through national diplomas, NVQs and A-levels to higher national diplomas, bachelors degrees, masters degrees and doctorates. In this chapter we take a look at the qualifications you can get below degree level and in subsequent chapters we investigate qualifications at first degree and above.

A recent survey of over 820,000 people in the industry by the Information Technology Industry Training Organisation (ITITO) discovered that 232,000 (28%) of IT practitioners have a first degree as their highest qualification, and 58,000 (7%) possess a postgraduate degree. Some 80,000 people (10%) have a higher national diploma; 90,000 (12%) went into the industry with A-levels and 107,000 (15%) got into IT with no more than GCSEs.

There is a strong message here. If you are determined to make your career in IT and the Internet there are many levels at which you can join. Some people start their career with minimal qualifications and work their way up to a job that suits their abilities. Others first study to gain a broader and deeper understanding of IT before getting a job in this multifaceted industry. Both methods are possible, though it is true to say that those who reach the most senior levels usually have graduate qualifications.

CITY & GUILDS OF LONDON INSTITUTE

The CGLI has developed over 70 different modules that relate to IT and the Internet. These modules can be studied in further education colleges and with private training providers throughout the UK. Each module develops your skill in something quite specific. Topics covered by these studies can be divided into five groups:

- increasing your proficiency in the use of a piece of software
- learning to program computers in a certain language
- electronics and methods needed to maintain certain pieces of equipment

- using the Internet
- office skills.

It is quite clear from the description of each module what you will be able to do when you have completed it.

In the first category are courses on word-processing and database methods, spreadsheets and desktop publishing. Modules in the second category cover 'coding and programming' in all the important computer programming languages including C, C++, COBOL, PASCAL and Visual Basic. On the hardware side of IT are courses in digital electronics, microprocessors, electronic printer installation, analogue circuits and fault diagnosis.

For those who want to use the Internet there are courses in 'Using the Internet' and 'Web page design'. The first teaches people how to connect to the Internet and the World Wide Web and how to use it to access and retrieve information. Students learn how to use e-mail, send and receive messages and the use of Internet 'browser' software. The second course covers everything that goes to make up a web page and the programming languages such as HTML and Java that are used to construct them. Students learn how to improve the presentation of their page by using graphics and how to link their web pages to other Internet sites. Because IT and the Internet are developing and changing so rapidly new modules are regularly added to the list, providing the means to keep your skills abreast of the latest technology. No previous qualifications are required and the courses do not assume that you have any knowledge of the subject when you begin.

A course is offered where you can learn how to install a computer system and another gives students the expertise to connect their system to the Internet via a telephone network and details of how to organise a local area network of computers.

In the 'office skills' category are modules on health and safety, paper handling, customer care and office practice.

Some of the modules can be taken in sequence to increase one's knowledge and skills in a particular subject. There are, for example, two modules on Programming in C, one at a more advanced level than the other. Students can put together several modules to gain a certificate, diploma or advanced diploma. These include the certificates given in the table below.

Qualifications from City & Guilds of London Institute

	Certificate	Diploma	Advanced diploma
Information technology	✔	✔	✔
Electronic systems	✔	✔	✔
Electronics and computer systems	✔	✔	✔
Information processing	✔		
Computer programming	✔		
Electronics servicing	✔		
Electronic office systems maintenance	✔		

OXFORD, CAMBRIDGE & RSA EXAMINATIONS

The Royal Society of Arts, with a long history of accrediting skills-related vocational courses, recently merged with the Oxford and Cambridge Examining Board to become OCR. Several IT-related courses of study are available at different levels of difficulty. They include studies that teach the basic IT skills right through to courses for IT practitioners. There are National Vocational Qualifications (NVQs), CLAIT (computer literacy and information technology) and the diploma and certificate in IT. These qualifications are grouped into different levels of difficulty, from entry level through levels 1, 2 and 3 to level 4. NVQs cover the following subjects:

- using IT
- developing IT programs
- developing IT systems
- operating IT systems
- installing and supporting IT systems
- teleworking
- managing IT for teleworking
- managing IT systems.

These are available in several strands for IT users, business IT and IT practitioners plus courses for those who wish to train students in IT.

There are qualifications in word-processing, desktop publishing and using the Internet. Internet Technologies Stage I assesses students' ability to use the Internet for communication, information gathering and publishing. Successful candidates can compose and edit a web page, use electronic mail and navigate the World Wide Web for research purposes.

EDEXCEL AND SCOTTISH QUALIFICATIONS AUTHORITY

Turning to courses that are more academic in nature, in the sense that they provide a broader knowledge of IT and the Internet as well as specific skills, we start with GCSEs and A-levels. Several examining boards set the curricula for GCSEs and A-levels. Schools and colleges quite often provide courses in subjects from different examining boards. Of those boards offering studies relating to IT, for example, Edexcel offers GCSEs and A-levels in Information Technology.

Although these subjects are available from the examining boards you may well discover that they are not taught in your local school. These qualifications are not a prerequisite for making a career in IT and the Internet, and while some schools teach them others do not.

Those who want to make their career in the engineering side of this subject, and progress their education via the GCSE and A-level route, will find that developing expertise in physics and mathematics will enable them to gain a place on an engineering degree course later. Those destined for the software side of the business still find that proficiency in maths is important, but require less knowledge of physics.

IT and the Internet offers so many different opportunities that there are also careers available to those who have not studied the subject to A-level, though a good GCSE in maths is always an advantage.

Finally there is the BTEC and SCOTVEC route. Edexcel offers studies that lead to GCSEs and BTEC NVQs in Information Technology. Studies resulting in qualifications of national and higher national diplomas and certificates in information technology are also available. While the lower range of these qualifications can be achieved by study at a college of further education the newer universities (see the Universities Central Admissions Service *Handbook*) also offer HND courses. All of these courses are highly practical and the development of skills is a central issue throughout.

The Scottish Qualifications Authority accredits courses in computing studies and information systems from Access level through intermediate and higher to advanced higher qualifications. Scottish Vocational Qualifications (SVQs) are also offered in exactly the same subjects that OCR covers. Additionally there are courses leading to the Higher National Diploma in: Computing – software development; Computing – support.

On the hardware side of IT there are also national and higher national certificates and diploma qualifications in: Electronics; Telecommunications; Computer Technology; Electronics Manufacturing.

Chapter 8
QUALIFICATIONS IN IT: DEGREE COURSES

Universities and colleges of higher education provide a plethora of degree courses that relate directly to information technology. Some have the words 'information technology' in their titles while others don't. It is an area in which the scope for misunderstanding is high and our purpose here is to unravel the subject, and clarify the options, by discussing each facet of information technology in turn.

The studies can be divided into two basic areas. First are the courses that lead to technical careers in the electronics and software side of information technology. These are for those who wish to make their career in the areas of researching, designing, developing, producing and testing IT systems. Second are those courses through which you learn how to apply these technologies to many of life's problems – running businesses, storing and distributing information, teaching information technology and much more.

For more information on specific courses consult *Computer Science Courses 2001* (published by UCAS/Trotman), the UCAS *Big Guide* and *Degree Course Offers* (published by Trotman).

HARDWARE

We begin with the technical courses. Some provide the basis for working in the electronics side of information technology, often known as the hardware, and are most often described as 'Electronic and Electrical Engineering'. Yet there is much more to information technology than electronics, for it includes telecommunications and networks. We shall discover later in this chapter a range of courses with other, quite different titles that relate to this particular strand.

SOFTWARE

Next are the degree studies that concentrate on software. Many of these are described as 'Computer Science' or 'Software Engineering'. Again there are ranges of related courses that have other titles, and these are also discussed later.

It is inevitable, given the dramatic growth of the Internet, the increasing range of services that it brings and the potential for so much more, that degrees in Internet studies would become available. Ten universities already run Internet degree courses and two offer a Higher National Diploma course in Web Site Management.

Given the sheer diversity of the subject you would not expect any undergraduate course to cover the entire area of all that there is to know about information technology. Yet 37 universities and 13 colleges of higher education do offer undergraduate studies in information technology. Each 'information technology' course emphasises certain areas of the subject and neglects others. The differences between the content of these courses are often greater than the similarities. It is always essential to read the prospectus of each institution in detail and, if necessary, speak to the admissions tutors at the universities to which you consider applying about the content of each course and the optional subjects that you can choose to study within it.

The course in business management and information technology at Greenwich School of Management, for example, is about the application of information technology to the management of business. That offered by St Martin's College, Lancaster, on information and communications technology education leads to qualified teacher status to teach information technology in primary schools.

There are so many applications of information technology and it is so all-pervading that there is plenty of scope for courses that focus primarily on its application in different settings. Among these are those dedicated to the use of information technology in business and those that concern themselves primarily with information management. Application of IT in the arts, especially the media, is another growing strand and courses in that area concentrate on multimedia systems, media communication and electronic graphics. Occupying the opposite end of the IT spectrum to electronics, these courses are designed for the artistically inclined student who wants to use all the latest IT techniques to develop their creative skills.

ELECTRONICS AND TELECOMMUNICATIONS

Just as essential in any IT system as computers, with their microprocessors and modems, memory storage discs and the rest, are the methods of transmitting information from place to place using radio waves, transmitters, waveguides and aerials or land lines. If you want to be involved in the demanding area of designing, making, testing and maintaining ever more powerful equipment the electronics route into an IT career is the one to choose. You will be working with such items as the next generation of mobile phones, computers, memory devices, fax machines, pagers and every other piece of equipment that is absolutely necessary for the application of information technology.

Most universities offer undergraduate studies in electronics. Many still cover both electrical and electronic engineering while some specialise in electronics. Sixty universities run degree courses in communications or telecommunications engineering; 32 offer degree courses in computer systems engineering; 8 offer studies in the relatively new technology of opto-electronics.

Course content

What would you be studying if you were an undergraduate on one of these courses? In your first year you will study the fundamentals of electronics, including electricity and magnetism, the physics of electronics, both logic and electronic circuits. The fundamentals of analogue and digital electronics will be in the curriculum and you might be introduced to integrated circuits. About a day each week is spent in the laboratory assembling and testing different circuits and coming to grips with the results of changing their components. Mathematics is an essential ingredient.

From studying the fundamentals, students move on in the second year to attempt projects that illustrate important aspects of the subject. At some stage semiconductor devices and signal processing will be covered; radio communications is also on the agenda. Students begin to tackle design projects and master the techniques used in the testing of a range of systems.

Progressing into the third year students are usually given the choice of several options. Many departments offer a range of courses such as electronic and integrated circuits, computer electronics and robotics and medical electronics.

The first two years of all these courses of study are often the same for everyone in the electrical engineering department and it is in the later years of the course that these specialisms become important as students choose between several options. Speech processing and cellular mobile phone communications are increasingly among the subjects studied.

Modern communications systems often rely on optical systems based on laser technology and the use of optical fibres to replace copper wires. The two systems, using electrons and light, have to connect with each other. Opto-electronics is often among the possibilities for study in degree courses in electronics and the University of Essex offers a course in optical communications.

THE SOFTWARE ROUTE

All information technology systems need software. It may be the kind of software we all use, such as word-processing and computer games, known as applications software. Even more important is the software that helps computers and other equipment to work and communicate with each other, called systems software. Often this is embedded in the electronic circuit and called upon to help a computer system or network to make a range of decisions. Many of the people who decide to get into information technology by the software route take a degree in computer science or software engineering. While computer science covers everything from programming to the architecture of computers and networks, software engineering is simply a highly structured method for writing computer programs so that they are readily updated and maintained. Courses in software engineering therefore focus on programming but include much more, especially the application of software to industrial and commercial problems.

Most universities offer degree courses in computer science; 58 have courses of study in software engineering; 22 offer degrees in computer systems and 23 run undergraduate courses on computer networks. Earlier we saw that many electrical engineering departments in universities run a range of courses and the first year or two are common. In computer science departments there are often several different degree courses that all have the study of some subjects in common. The difference between a software engineering course and a computer science degree may only be in the final-year options.

Course content

As an example we chose the Department of Computer Science at Warwick University. It offers courses in computer science and computer systems engineering plus a range of courses in collaboration with other departments. These include computer and management science and computer and business studies.

Students in the first year of computer science study such subjects as sequential programming, which includes information structures, abstract data types and functional programming plus courses in computer organisation and mathematics. They are also introduced to computer organisation and architecture as well as the structure of computer systems. At this stage they become familiar with machine code and a range of software tools. Even in the initial stages of the course they can choose two courses from a variety of options.

Entering the second year, systematic software development is on the menu. Automata and formal languages, logic and the theoretical foundations of programming languages are also among the courses studied. It is at this stage that the concept of software engineering is introduced – how software is developed and how database systems are designed and used. Computer systems are studied in detail.

In the final year students have a vast range of options to choose from. They include artificial intelligence, compiler design, computer graphics, mobile robot technology and the architecture of integrated circuits.

Students on the computer systems engineering course study some of the above subjects but their development is much more biased towards electronics. First-year students are introduced to analogue electronics and the principles of electricity. They investigate computer architecture but like their computer science colleagues they also study programming and the design of information structures.

Moving into their second year control and communication is on the curriculum together with engineering design and software engineering. Topics such as digital signal processing, automation and robotics, data communications networks and systematic software development are studied at this stage.

Projects are the key to success in the third year and they are linked to the research interests of the department or of nearby companies. Expert systems, artificial intelligence and computer graphics are among the large array of subjects studied by past students. Completion of these three years of study leads to a BEng degree.

To become a professional chartered engineer it is now necessary to be educated to masters degree level (see Chapter 9) and Warwick is among many universities that offer an additional year for the Master of Engineering degree in Computer Systems Engineering. The four-year programme includes additional studies in business subjects including starting a business, industrial law, operational research and the management of technology.

At UMIST by contrast the degree programmes offered by the department of computing are information systems engineering, computer science, software engineering and computer systems engineering. Also on the menu are artificial intelligence, neuroscience and computation plus management and information technology. The department focuses its efforts on the 'application of information technology' rather than the 'development of fundamental computing technologies'.

DEGREES IN INFORMATION TECHNOLOGY

Degree studies in information technology are much broader than the more specialist courses discussed above. Some, like the course at the University of Teesside, stress the application of information technology rather than the fundamental engineering technologies that underpin it.

Course content

Students in their first year of study are introduced to the fundamentals of communications, the principles of software, systems design. They begin to understand systems analysis and the principles of computers. They are also introduced to business organisation.

Entering their second year of study students take a close look at management information systems and databases. They investigate the interface between IT systems and the user and study networks and communication systems. In parallel with these courses they also begin to master object-oriented computer programming, a relatively new type of programming that includes such languages as C and C++ (see applications programmer on page 6).

In common with many degree courses in information technology the students at Teesside take a year out in industry during their third year to see how information technology is used in practice and gain a detailed understanding of the career opportunities.

The final year of this course includes the investigation of networks of computers and the development of information systems. As in most technology-based degree courses, students must complete a project. They can also choose between a range of options including artificial intelligence, computer graphics, expert systems and neural networks.

Throughout their studies students have the opportunity to learn a European language and to investigate business and financial IT systems.

At the University of Lincolnshire and Humberside the emphasis is slightly different. Information technology is available as a joint honours degree with any of 13 different subjects. The IT part of the course focuses on 'the practical application and improvement of available tools and techniques to provide realistic solutions to a wide range of contemporary and social issues'. This includes studies of business systems, IT applications and problem solving, the development of end-user applications and communication principles. It includes database systems networks and the design of user interfaces. As the studies reach an advanced stage students investigate the acquisition and evaluation of IT systems, and the development of successful IT strategies in business.

IT IN BUSINESS

Business and IT are now so firmly intertwined that the dividing lines have become blurred. IT is indispensable to business. There are many courses that prepare students for a career in business where they can apply their new-found knowledge of relevant information technology.

Five universities and colleges offer degrees in business communication: Bournemouth University, King Alfred's College Winchester, the London Institute, Staffordshire University and the University of Ulster. E-commerce is now a major growth area and a degree course in electronic business is offered at the University of Lincolnshire and Humberside. The University of Nottingham runs a course on digital business.

More institutions concentrate on teaching business systems. These are: Bradford College, University of West of England, Bristol, the Colchester Institute, Luton University, Middlesex University, University of Salford and Sheffield Hallam University. But many of the other courses in business and management include an element of IT or the possibility of taking options within the course that are concerned with IT. If your chosen career is towards management or in business do read the prospectuses carefully with an eye to the possibilities of learning something about modern business technology.

THE INTERNET

What is it like to study the Internet at university? The University of Essex is one of the institutions offering this type of course. It runs two degree programmes, one on Internet computing and the other on Internet engineering. In common with all the other IT-related degrees the course includes lectures, tutorials, problem classes and laboratory work.

Course content

Students on both courses study the same subjects in the first year. They include an introduction to Internet computing and networks, procedural programming and software engineering. Information engineering and computer engineering are also among the topics to be studied.

After that students on the Internet computing course gain practical experience of designing and writing web applications. For this they learn the Java language. They discover how to design and write search engines that source the vast resources of the Internet for information. Software robots, known as 'softbots', are used to go out and search for specific topics and asked to report back what they have discovered. Students are introduced to these.

By contrast the emphasis on the Internet engineering course is more towards the engineering of the Internet, especially computer networks. Students learn how to develop application software that can be used on the Internet. Topics investigated in the final year include servers and crawlers, multilevel databases, networked virtual reality and autonomous agents.

It's a great new world and none of us can predict where these new technologies will lead in ten or 20 years' time, but students on these courses will be at the forefront of the Internet revolution.

CHOOSING A COURSE

Clearly the choice of courses in IT is extremely wide. No two courses are the same and it is essential to read the prospectus of each course in detail. It helps if you have a strong idea of what you would like to do when you have completed the course. The more technical courses can lead to a career in the design and development of hardware and are for those with a practical bent who enjoy working with and improving equipment. A-levels, or their equivalent, in physics and maths are often demanded for entry into these.

Students with meticulous attention to detail and a logical approach, who wish to avoid practical work, might consider the software route.

If, however, your interest is in business and the application of information technology in a commercial or industrial setting, those degree studies that concentrate on the application of IT in business are perhaps a better option.

Entrance requirements

Entrance requirements vary considerably from one course to another. You need to take a view on whether you are likely to obtain the minimum qualifications for the course and whether you can compete for a place on a very popular degree.

Some, though not all, of the universities take a hard look at your maths GCSE result and expect it to be good. Quite a few of the degree courses, though not by any means all, look for an A or B at A-level in maths. After that the entrance requirements are extremely varied, from three As at A-level at Cambridge, down to two As and a B at Birmingham, Manchester, Nottingham, Warwick and Oxford. Following these there is a wide spectrum of degree course requirements, right down to ten UCAS points.

In electronics more emphasis is given to physics – Warwick, for example, look for an A or B. Consult the UCAS *Big Guide* and *Degree Course Offers* (published by Trotman) for the full details.

59

APPLYING FOR A PLACE

All universities are members of the Universities and Colleges Admissions Service and prospective students must apply through UCAS, Rosehill, New Barn Lane, Cheltenham, Gloucestershire GL52 3LZ, tel 01242 227788. UCAS has a web site that can be consulted at www.ucas.com. You can telephone UCAS to request an application form and the UCAS *Handbook*, which contains a great deal of useful information. Applications should be made between 1st September and 15th December.

GETTING TO KNOW THE CAMPUSES

If you are considering going to live at a university for three years or more you should, if possible, visit the campus and see if you feel at home. Many universities run open days, details of which are available from each individual department. When visiting departments that run IT-related courses it is always useful to enquire about the access students have to computers. Is this freely available or is it rationed? In some universities every student has access to a computer at all times, in others various rota systems operate, giving students access in turn to scarce resources.

Many universities invite prospective students for interview with the admissions tutor and possibly other members of the department. The event usually includes a departmental tour. To be successful it is essential to go prepared. Read about the department in the prospectus and look up their web page on the Internet. Express an interest in the content of the course and the options that are available and, if you can, illustrate your interest by things you have done at school or in your leisure time. You cannot expect success in an interview for a place on an Internet course, for example, if you appear never to have used it and have no interest in it. Expect to be asked about your own experiences.

Chapter 9
QUALIFICATIONS IN IT: POSTGRADUATE STUDIES

There are two fundamental reasons why students study for higher degrees in information technology and related subjects. The first is to move their career into information technology when it was previously heading in a different direction; the second is to study one area of information technology in detail having first completed a relevant undergraduate degree. We will look at each in turn and the opportunities that are available.

MOVING INTO IT

Quite often these days there are graduates who took a degree quite unrelated to information technology and, on discovering the astonishing range of career opportunities described in this book, decide that they will move their career in that direction. There are several ways of doing this, one of which is to complete some of the City & Guilds or OCR courses, details of which were given in Chapter 7.

Another is to complete one of the numerous courses at postgraduate level that lead to a diploma or a masters degree and help graduates to convert into information technologists. Studies include lectures, tutorials and practical work, case studies and applications of the technology to specific problems. The diploma courses start in September and end after an examination in June. Masters courses in the same subject and in the same department are identical in their initial content but additionally include the completion of a project and the writing of a thesis. This extends the course to a full calendar year. While many of these courses are taken by full-time study, a good proportion can be completed on a part-time basis.

A few are organised specially for a range of local employers and involve attendance at university for a day each week for the duration of the studies.

The Engineering and Physical Sciences Research Council (EPSRC) supports study in this area with financial awards and the payment of fees. At the time of writing there were 48 postgraduate IT conversion courses throughout the UK on which some students received support from the EPSRC. Around 900 students receive awards each year. However, not everyone attending these courses is lucky enough to obtain this funding. Applicants must have at least a lower second-class honours degree and be British nationals. European Union nationals can receive a 'fees only' award.

Typical of these conversion courses is the masters degree in information technology at De Montfort University (Milton Keynes). An honours degree in any discipline is required. 'Graduates from non-technical backgrounds must demonstrate an ability to absorb technical ideas'. Studies include the basics of programming, of computer hardware and systems, and researching the ways in which humans and computers interface with each other. The structure and configuration of public and private communications networks and distributed systems are also included. Software engineering is also on the agenda. It covers the specification, design and construction of software. The important area of databases is also covered.'

The range of applications of information technology covered by the course includes robotics, knowledge-based systems, voice and image processing and electronic mail. For their projects many students work closely with industrial and commercial organisations to apply information technology in a real business situation.

Another example is the conversion course in information technology at Queen Mary & Westfield College, London. This course divides students into two streams – those who will tackle electronics and those who stick to the software. Subjects studied include programming, computer systems, microelectronics, databases, computer communication, human–computer interfaces, artificial intelligence and knowledge-based systems.

Several courses are offered that relate IT to business. Middlesex University provides an MSc in Business Information Technology and there is one at Manchester University on Business Information Systems. Salford and Strathclyde universities both offer courses in the management of information systems.

Masters courses are also available on the many different aspects of information technology. UK universities offer around 300 diploma or masters-taught courses in computer sciences. Some of these are simply called computer science, others software engineering. There are courses in information systems management. But there are also more specialist courses. Sheffield University offers a course in textual computing and Nottingham University has a course in musicology – the application of IT to music.

Some of these courses are more demanding than others in their requirements for previous qualifications. While many take students with a degree in any subject and assume no prior knowledge, others restrict their intake to scientists, engineers and mathematicians.

The masters course at Imperial College, for example, in foundations of advanced information technology, requires applicants to have a degree in computer science, information technology, maths or a related subject.

MOVING ON IN IT

Those who already possess qualifications in IT, computer science and related disciplines can use postgraduate study to specialise in one area of the subject. Courses in virtual reality, artificial intelligence, robotics, multimedia and other specialist areas are also available.

Similarly on the electronics and hardware side of the business many universities offer postgraduate studies in specialist areas. About 45 courses of study are available in control systems and related subjects and 160 in studies relating to electronics. These include advanced courses on microprocessors, telecommunications, digital electronics, semiconductor devices, VLSI (see integrated circuit designer, page 12), opto-electronics, process control, satellite engineering, data communications and networks, broadband phonetic networks and many other IT topics. Most of these subjects are mentioned in other parts of this book, either as a part of undergraduate degree studies or as areas in which employers recruit. These have a value for those who want to become specialist engineers in one particular area of the IT industry and they all require aspiring applicants to possess relevant qualifications.

Our advice is to take a very close look at the content of any course you consider taking and be absolutely sure that it not only gives you a better knowledge of IT but also develops the essential skills you need to make a career in this fast-developing field. Skills in computer programming, especially in object-oriented languages, an understanding of operating systems and software – especially databases, word processing and spreadsheets – can always be used to attract employers. An understanding of networks, servers and the tools required to make them operational is another area that makes postgraduates attractive to employees. Make sure that your course will help you to develop these skills before you spend nine months or more of your valuable time pursuing it.

RESEARCH DEGREES

In addition to the advanced masters courses there are also opportunities for students to gain higher degrees by research. Again the EPSRC finances much of the research carried out in this area. Research degrees can lead to an MSc, MPhil or PhD. A rule of thumb is that an MSc is given for one year's research, an MPhil for two and a PhD for three or more. Researchers investigate a particular topic in detail and conclude their studies by writing a thesis.

Typical of the subjects studied in information technology are the human/computer interface, digital communications, intelligent systems and policy issues relating to the effect of IT on society.

At Southampton University scientists are studying financial information systems for banking and accounting. Security has become an essential ingredient now that so many applications are emerging in e-commerce. You are not going to give a computer your credit card details unless you feel secure about it. PhD students at Leicester are among those investigating security management and information technology.

Research on the hardware side of IT includes projects in microelectronics and microprocessors, communications, information engineering and semiconductors. It is all at the leading edge of this rapidly changing technology so who can say where it will lead? For some this is quite an exciting prospect.

Chapter 10
PROFESSIONAL BODIES

When you're working in IT and the Internet, joining a professional body and thus developing your expertise, meeting likeminded professionals and working towards a professional qualification will help you to develop your career. Not everyone in the IT industry is a member of a professional body – some employers strongly encourage their staff to join one and other don't. Yet there are good reasons for becoming a member of one of the relevant professional bodies that serve the IT industry.

They all provide regular newsletters or magazines that keep you in touch with the latest professional issues. Many have schemes that help people new to the industry with their training and professional development, leading eventually to full recognition as a professional. Such schemes provide a structure against which you can develop your skills. Even if a professional qualification is not seen as important to your employer it will be a valuable asset when you decide that the time has come to move on.

The institutions that represent people working in IT and the Internet are:

- the British Computer Society
- the Institute for the Management of Information Systems
- the Institution of Analysts and Programmers
- the Institution of Electrical Engineers
- the Institution of Incorporated Engineers.

The first three institutions listed are primarily concerned with software professionals and the last two with those whose skills are in electronics, but there is often considerable overlap between the two.

The larger institutions have branches around the UK that hold regular meetings on topics of mutual interest. They hold regular conferences on relevant topics and promote specialist interest groups that provide the opportunity to meet other professionals with similar interests to your own.

THE ENGINEERING COUNCIL

The Engineering Council oversees the professional qualifications of engineers and sets the standards required to reach the grades of engineering technician, incorporated engineer and chartered engineer. Some of the institutions referred to in this chapter provide a route to these qualifications. The council has published its *Standards and Routes to Professional Qualifications*; they require incorporated engineers to gain bachelors degree-level qualifications and chartered engineers to reach masters degree level. In addition specified periods of training and professional experience are required.

THE BRITISH COMPUTER SOCIETY (BCS)

The British Computer Society is one of the most respected professional bodies in the field of IT. Its professional development scheme is based upon an industry-structured model that defines over 250 roles within the industry and the skills that are required to fulfil each of these roles professionally.

The broad areas it covers are:

- support and administration
- education and training
- customer relations
- quality
- technical advice and constancy
- service delivery
- systems development and maintenance
- policy planning and research
- management.

In the service delivery area, for example, there are 12 different roles:

- capacity management
- computer operations
- database administration
- hardware/software installation
- help desk
- network administration and support
- network control
- problem management
- service delivery planning and control
- service level monitoring
- systems programming
- user support.

If you look back to earlier chapters, particularly Chapter 1, you will discover that these are related to specific jobs in the industry. Within each occupation there are a range of tasks and by mastering these tasks trainees further their own development. A logbook is provided to record progress and completion of the scheme can lead to qualification as an incorporated or chartered engineer. Over 200 employers and 13 universities provide training that is accredited under the scheme. Look out for degree courses that are accredited by the BCS.

INSTITUTION OF INCORPORATED ENGINEERS (IIE)

The Institution of Incorporated Engineers is the leading institution for electronic engineers who aspire to the professional grade of incorporated engineer. A lively society, with a monthly journal, interest groups and branches all over the UK, it provides a meeting point and network facility for electronic engineers who are engaged in information technology plus many other areas of electronics. It maintains a telecommunications and information engineering special-interest group for members who are working in, or are keen to develop, their knowledge and skills in IT and Internet-related areas. The institution publishes a list of accredited degree courses.

INSTITUTION OF ELECTRICAL ENGINEERS (IEE)

One of the oldest of the engineering institutions, the IEE provides a route to chartered engineer status for electronic engineers. In common with all of the other institutions it encourages student membership, providing a series of lectures and special services to students. It maintains an industry group on multimedia communications and special-interest groups that meet to discuss electronics and communication and informatics. The institution accredits many of the four-year university courses that lead to an MEng degree and publishes a list of these. It also publishes the names of employers whose training schemes it approves.

INSTITUTE FOR THE MANAGEMENT OF INFORMATION SYSTEMS (IMIS)

IMIS is the professional body for managers of information systems. It has over 10,000 members and grades of membership from student member up to fellow. The institute publishes a monthly journal. There is a comprehensive education and training structure and currently over 6000 students in 58 countries worldwide are studying to complete its examinations that lead to corporate membership. The exams begin at the foundation level (equivalent to NVQ level 2) and move through diploma (equivalent to first-year university level) through to higher diploma and graduate. Several university degree courses are accredited by the IMIS and the degree in management of information systems offered by Greenwich University leads to full corporate membership.

INSTITUTION OF ANALYSTS AND PROGRAMMERS (IAP)

The IAP has 3000 members both in the UK and internationally. It encourages those on relevant courses of study to join as student members. Applicants are assessed on a system under which points are given for experience and training in programming, analysis and business. The institution publishes details of the experience and skills required for members to attain each grade of membership, from student through graduate, associate, member and fellow. Members can apply to move into a higher grade whenever their career has developed to a stage that meets the requirements.

FURTHER READING

Careers in Information Technology, published by Kogan Page

Careers in Multimedia, published by Ziff Davis

Complete Guide to Computer Science Courses 2001, published by UCAS/Trotman

Computing Careers Yearbook, published by VNU Publications

Computing your Career, published by Federation of Recruitment and Employment Services (FRES)

Degree Course Offers, published by Trotman

Focus on Information Technology, published by Central Services Unit

How to get a Job in Microcomputing, published by *Computer Weekly*

How to master psychometric tests, published by Kogan Page

How to succeed in psychometric tests, published by Sheldon Business Books

Information Technology, published by Cambridge Market Intelligence

IT and Communications Casebook, published by Hobsons

IT Business, published by GTI

Multimedia, published by Blueprint

New Media Companies, published by Waterflow

Studying Computer Science, Questions and Answers, degree subject guide, published by Trotman

University and College Entrance: The Official Guide, published by UCAS

Who's Who in IT, published by *Network Week*

Who's Who in UK Interactive Media, published by DP Media

Working in Electronics, published by COIC

Working in Information Technology, published by Careers and Occupational Information Centre (COIC)

USEFUL ADDRESSES

British Computer Society
1 Stanford Street
Swindon SN1 1HJ
Tel 01793 417417
www.bcs.org.uk

City & Guilds of London Institute
1 Guiltspur Street
London EC1A 9DD
Tel 020 7294 2800
www.city-and-guilds.co.uk

Computer Software and Services Association
20 Red Lion Street
London WC1R 4QN
Tel 020 7395 6700
www.cssa.co.uk

Edexcel
Stewart House
32 Russell Square
London WC1B 5DN
Tel 020 7393 4445
www.edexcel.org.uk

Information Technology National Training Organisation
16–18 Berners Street
London W1P 3DD
Tel 020 7580 6677

Institution of Electrical Engineers
Savoy Place
London WC2R 0BL
Tel 020 7240 1871
www.iee.org.uk

Oxford, Cambridge and RSA Examinations
Westwood Way
Coventry CV4 8JQ
Tel 024 7647 0033
www.ocr.org.uk

Scottish Qualifications Authority
Hanover House
24 Douglas Street
Glasgow G2 7NQ
Tel 0131 654 2664
www.sqa.org.uk

Universities and Colleges Admissions Service
Rosehill
New Barn Lane
Cheltenham
Gloucestershire GL52 3LZ
Tel 01242 227788
www.ucas.com